Animals in the...
Zoo

Siân Smith

Raintree

Raintree is an imprint of Capstone Global Library Limited, a company incorporated in England and Wales having its registered office at 7 Pilgrim Street, London, EC4V 6LB – Registered company number: 6695582

www.raintreepublishers.co.uk
myorders@raintreepublishers.co.uk

Edited by Siân Smith, John-Paul Wilkins and Helen Cox Cannons
Designed by Cynthia Akiyoshi
Picture research by Mica Brancic and Tracy Cummins
Production by Victoria Fitzgerald
Originated by Capstone Global Library
Printed and bound in China

ISBN 978 1 406 28050 0
18 17 16 15 14
10 9 8 7 6 5 4 3 2 1

British Library Cataloguing in Publication Data
A full catalogue record for this book is available from the British Library.

Acknowledgements
We would like to thank the following for permission to reproduce photographs: Shutterstock pp. 1 (© belizar), 2 (© MaZiKab), 3 left, 20 top middle (© Eric Isselee), 3 middle, 20 top right (© Talvi), 3 right, 20 top left (© Aaron Amat), 4 (© Andrey Burmakin), 5 (© Tomo), 6 (© Anan Kaewkhammul), 7 (© Lynn Whitt), 8 (© Galina Barskaya), 10 (© Fotokon), 11, 22b (© worldswildlifewonders), 12, 22a (© Anthony Cooper), 13 (© Nicola Colombo), 14 (© babetka), 15 (© lunatic67), 16 (© enciktat), 17, 21 (© Hung Chung Chih), 18 (© Seleznev Oleg), 19 (© tratong), 20 bottom left (© Vadim Petrakov), 20 bottom middle (© Villiers Steyn), 20 bottom right (© kanate).

Front cover photograph of a giraffe reproduced with kind permission of Shutterstock (© belizar).

Every effort has been made to contact copyright holders of material reproduced in this book. Any omissions will be rectified in subsequent printings if notice is given to the publisher.

Contents

Zoo animals 4

Animal homes 20

What am I? 21

Picture glossary 22

Index 22

Notes for teachers
    and parents 23

Word coverage 24

Zoo animals

Look at the elephant.

Look at the monkey.

Look at the tiger.

Look at the lion.

Look at the penguin.

Look at the seal.

Look at the polar bear.

Look at the giraffe.

Look at the koala.

Look at the crocodile.

Look at the hippo.

Look at the koala.

Look at the crocodile.

Look at the snake.

parrot

Look at the parrot.

Look at the panda.

Look at the camel.

meerkat

Look at the meerkat.

Animal homes

Where do these animals live in the wild?

meerkat

seal

elephant

grassland

desert

sea

What am I?

I have claws.

I eat bamboo.

I have two arms and two legs.

I am covered in black and white fur.

Answer: A panda.

Picture glossary

 **crocodile**

 **koala**

Index

crocodile 12

elephant 4

koala 11

lion 7

meerkat 19

panda 17

seal 9

snake 15

22

Notes for teachers and parents

Before reading

Tuning in: Talk about animals the child has seen at a zoo or on TV.
  Which animal has a trunk? Which animal roars?

After reading

Recall and reflection: Which animals have stripes? Which animal has a hump?
Sentence knowledge: Help the child to count the number of words in each
  sentence.
Word knowledge (phonics): Encourage the child to point at the word 'at' on
  any page. Sound out the phonemes in the word 'a/t'. Ask the child to sound
  out each letter as they point at it and then blend the sounds together to
  make the word 'get'.
Word recognition: Challenge the child to race you to point at the word 'the' on
  any page.

Rounding off

Play a rhyming game: How many words can you think of that rhyme with 'zoo'
  (shoe, you, too, do, blue) etc.?

Word coverage

Sentence stem

Look at the _____.

High-frequency words

at
look
the

**Ask children to read
these words:**

lion	p7
seal	p9
hippo	p13
panda	p17

Topic words

camel
crocodile
elephant
giraffe
hippo
koala
lion
meerkat
monkey
panda
parrot
penguin
polar bear
seal
snake
tiger